# Dedication

I dedicate this book to Lucy Maud Montgomery for being my favorite author, to all the other authors who have inspired me, to the Indigo Girls for their beautiful music that has helped me through many trials and tribulations, and finally, to every girl who has come before me or will come after me.

# Acknowledgments

There are many people who helped me with this book, and without their help I probably wouldn't have made it.

Thank you to my English teachers Kate and Cindy for reading through many rough drafts and giving me their comments and ideas. Thank you to my parents for putting up with my moods and for all around spoiling and loving me.

Thanks also to my friends who saw the beginnings of the book in sixth grade (a language arts assignment). I figured since I knew a lot about journal-writing, I would make a book about journaling for my friends to fill in. It was ten pages long, illustrated by me, and printed out on my home computer. It's come a long way since then! I thank my friends for telling me what they liked and didn't like about it.

Thank you to Dr. Raymond B. Weiss for reviewing the medical information in "Growing Up." Also, thank you to my public library for letting me come in so many times and check out and photocopy as many things as I wanted.

# Contents

# Introduction

*Totally Private & Personal* is a book of journaling ideas for girls and young women ages 11–16. If you are a precocious ten-year-old or a young adult who likes to journal, there's probably something in here for you, too.

I wrote this book because I know how it feels to be a teenage girl (I am one). Often things seem very confusing, and your self-esteem may take a nose-dive. One minute you feel on top of the world, the next you feel like everyone's against you. You worry about lots of things: parents (can't live with 'em, can't live without 'em), boys (can't live with 'em, don't want to live without 'em), plus school, friends, body changes, and more.

It seems like one day you're running around outdoors and scraping your knees, and the next day you've got a FIGURE and are worrying about which outfit looks good on you. (Well, maybe it doesn't happen that fast but you get the idea.) What I mean to say is that I wrote this book because I was wishing someone had written it for me.

There are many good reasons for keeping a journal at this stage in your life and forever. It's a good release when you're angry, sad, troubled, or even wonderfully happy. It's your safe haven for exploring your feelings and dreams. The things you write in your journal can inspire you now and always. You can record your thoughts and memories (so that one day far from now you're able to reread your old journals and exclaim, "Ah, youth!"), and you can tell your life story. The most important thing you'll ever write is your journal, even if it's not the best thing you ever write.

All you need to get started on your journal is a desire to get your thoughts on paper and something to write in. Record your thoughts, feelings, impressions, likes, dislikes, favorites, problems, and anything else you're in the mood to think and write about. I've included some of my own journal entries for you to read, so you can see the different ways I use my journal. But don't feel that you have to write like me!

Journals aren't just for writing. You can put photos in your journal, as well as cartoons, letters from friends, ticket stubs from a favorite play, or anything else that means something to you. Throughout this book, you'll find ideas, suggestions, advice, and tips for keeping a fun and creative journal. Some of the ideas are based on the seasons and holidays, others are fine for any time of year. Use the suggestions any way you want—you can go in order or you can skip around.

Along the way, you'll also find other kinds of activities and advice. Because this book was written for girls and young women, I've added some special sections about growing up and feeling great about being a girl. I've also included lots of resources (recommended books, magazines, and Web sites) that are helpful, fun, and informative.

To quote Shakespeare: "The pen is mightier than the sword." That is a true statement. My advice is to always use your pens well. Write from your heart, and voice your opinions. Whether ballpoint or felt-tip, quill or fountain, the pen is a powerful tool.

If you would like to write to me about your journaling experiences, this book, or anything else that's on your mind, I'd like to hear from you. You can write to me at this address:

> Jessica Wilber
> c/o Free Spirit Publishing Inc.
> 400 First Avenue North, Suite 616
> Minneapolis, MN 55401-1730

Or contact me by E-mail:

> FRFV51B@prodigy.com

I wish you a fun and rewarding journaling experience. Good luck!

Jessica Wilber
Racine, Wisconsin

# 2 Rules

There are only two rules
for journal-keeping:

**1.** Date every entry.

**2.** Don't make any more rules.

# Getting Ready to Journal

There are a few things you can do to get ready to journal. First, tell yourself that journaling is fun. Don't worry about the quality of your writing or about making mistakes on the page. Spelling and grammar don't have to matter when you are journaling.

Next, think of how you can personalize your journaling. You might pick a special time and place for writing. Or you might always use the same kind of pen. It's up to you!

# Choosing Your Journal

Choosing a journal is a very personal thing. Your journal can be big or small, thick or thin. You might like a typical diary, with lines for writing on and printed dates. Or you might prefer a blank book (lined or unlined), a spiral notebook, a hardbound or accordion-style book, or even loose-leaf paper in a folder or three-ring binder.

Another idea is to try recording your private thoughts using a tape recorder or video camera. (It's fun to watch yourself on tape or listen to your voice—especially a few months or a year later!)

Here are some other things to think about when choosing your journal:

* Writing utensils you'll use (pen, pencil, markers—what color?)

* Art supplies (optional—try crayons, calligraphy pens, rubber stamps, colored pencils, etc.)

* Other fun items (glitter, stickers, a camera and film—go crazy!).

# Finding Time to Journal

You can pick up your journal and write in it any time, day or night. What works best for you? Do you like to write in the morning before school? At night before you go to bed? Sunday afternoons only? I sometimes go for several days without writing in my journal (TIP: Don't feel guilty about it!)

How much time do you want to spend on each journal entry? My rule of thumb is "as long as I feel like." Sometimes I'll write for a few minutes, sometimes much longer.

Try not to force yourself to write for a certain amount of time (say a half hour) unless that seems to work best for you. Some writers like to time themselves, others like to have as much freedom as possible. Be flexible.

# Privacy

Because journal-writing is a personal thing, it's important to have a special place, privacy, and alone time. If you want, make a "Do Not Disturb" sign for the door of your bedroom or have a special signal. For example, a blue ribbon looped around the doorknob could mean "Talk to me later." Ask your family members to respect your alone time (for writing a Privacy Contract, see page 135).

I have different times and places that I prefer, depending on the mood I'm in. Usually I sit on my bed, but sometimes I sit on my window seat and look outside. At Christmastime, I like to wait until no one else is around, then sit by the glowing Christmas tree. In spring and early fall, I sit on the roof of our garage or take a tape recorder with me on a bike ride, record my thoughts, and later transcribe them to paper.

Journaling is a very personal, sacred thing, so try to treat it that way. Protect the privacy of your journaling time as carefully as you protect your most private thoughts. I suggest finding a quiet place where you won't be interrupted, but the rest is up to you. You can sit wherever you want and make your place special however you like. If you want to light candles, listen to music, or sit with your toes in the river, do just that.

*"A writer needs certain conditions in which to work and create art. She needs a piece of time; peace of mind; a quiet place; and a private life."*

Margaret Walker in *The Writer on Her Work*

# Your Personal Writing Spot

You can design a personal writing spot for yourself—an area where you write, think, and relax, or even laugh and dance.

Many female writers and book heroines have had personal writing spots. For instance, Jo March in Louisa May Alcott's *Little Women* always wrote in her garret with her nightcap on and her pet rat, Scrabble, by her side. Or what about L. M. Montgomery's *Emily of New Moon?* Emily wrote in her attic and put her private writings on a hidden shelf—at least they were private until her aunt found them! My friend Alison sits by her window or at her computer to write. My friend Monica sits on her bed. Lots of people have personal writing spots and you should, too!

Here's how to create a personal writing spot in your own bedroom:

* Change the lighting. Choose white lights (very elegant and cheery), lightbulbs in your favorite color (personalized), or strings of lights with special designs (chili peppers, moons, suns, cows, flowers, seashells, or M&M's).

* Redesign the walls. Choose wallpaper, a border that you like, or paint (maybe

even black, camouflage, stripes, spirals, or scenes). My personal favorite scenes are under-the-sea, rainforest, and medieval times. Ask your parents first, though!

* Turn your bed into a special place. Add a canopy or mosquito netting, or try a bunk bed.

* Have a writing chair. This can be your desk chair (add a comfy cushion, if you want), a soft chair, a lawn chair, even a window seat—anything goes!

* Add wall coverings. Hang hand-drawn pictures or put up posters of your favorite stars, places you want to go or have been, or ones with messages you like. Hang a bulletin board to display your awards, photos, souvenirs, postcards, and drawings.

* Create a storage space. You can decorate a box to hide favorite books, writing tools, and pictures of your friends and family. Have a special drawer for snacks.

# Naming Your Journal

Many people name their journals and you can, too. Anne Frank—the young Jewish girl who hid from the Nazis during World War II and recorded all her thoughts in a diary—named hers Kitty. Zlata Filipovic, at age 11, started keeping a diary of her experience in war-torn Sarajevo. She called her diary Mimmy.

Like Anne and Zlata, I decided to name my journals. One is Princess Dido, after a main character in a story I wrote. Another is Alison, after my best friend. My third journal is Victoria. A friend of mine called her journal Faith. To name yours, just write down a possible list of names and pick the one you like best.

## A Promise to Yourself

*I do solemnly swear to keep my journal*
*forever and to read it when I grow up.*

*Anne Frank: The Diary of a Young Girl* by Anne Frank (NY: Bantam Books, Inc., 1993). Anne's beautiful diary is about a young girl's courage. She describes the joys and torments of day-to-day life during her two years of hiding in an attic in Nazi-occupied Holland.

*Zlata's Diary* by Zlata Filipovic (NY: Viking Penguin, 1995). Zlata's life was like that of most young girls, until the bombs started falling in Sarajevo. Confined to her family's apartment, she pours out her heart to her diary. She describes the violence, the shortages of food and water, and her struggle to live a normal life.

# From My Journal

*March 12, 1994 (Saturday)*

*Dear Diary,*

*It is 1:25 P.M. You know how Anne Frank and Zlata Filipovic named their diaries something? Well, I'm going to name YOU something!*

*Here are some ideas: Victoria, Anthea, Zoe, Trissy, Mercy, Anne, Emily, Zlata, Marcie, Faith, Spring, April, Molly, Felicity, Addy, or Lily. I've decided on Victoria....*

*Love,*
*Jessica*

# The Day You Begin

Write a description of who you are today, right now. Or make a collage of this day. Include newspaper headlines, a photo or drawing of yourself, your horoscope, weather notes, etc. Or have a party in your honor (celebrate life, love, and yourself) and write about it.

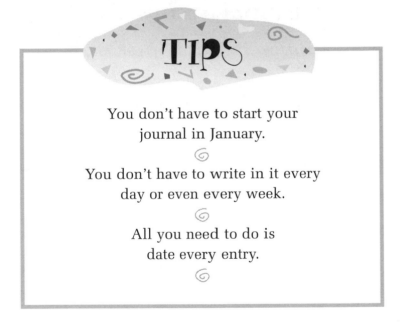

## TIPS

You don't have to start your
journal in January.

You don't have to write in it every
day or even every week.

All you need to do is
date every entry.

> *"Journal writing is a voyage into the interior."*

Christina Baldwin in *One to One*

# A Journal About You

Your journal is about you. It's a place to explore how you feel, who you are, and what you'll be when you grow up.

Don't hold back when you write—let it all out! (Remember, you're the only one reading your journal, so don't worry about what other people might think.) Use your journal to share your secret dreams, wishes, and goals. Following are some ideas for looking inside yourself.

# Who You Are

Answer this question, "Who are you?" Try to think of what makes you unique and write about it in your journal. You can make a list that describes your personality traits, your likes and dislikes, and so on.

Or, if you have more time, try writing a mini-autobiography in your journal. Write about your life, your family and friends, your school, your talents, things you believe in, and anything else that's important to you.

You could include funny stories about your childhood or the story of the day you were born. How about your most memorable day or moment?

Now answer this question, "Who do you want to be?" (I don't mean other than yourself, I mean in the future.) Do you want to be an astronaut, a writer, an athlete, a scientist...? In the future, what will be different about you and what will stay the same?

# Your Goals

Goals give you something to reach for. One way to keep track of your goals is by writing them in your journal, like I do. Make a list of five goals (long-term and short-term) and refer back to them every once in a while.

If you are having trouble meeting your personal goals, try to figure out why. What's holding you back?

For example, do you have enough free time for focusing on yourself—time away from school, extra-curricular activities, chores? Or are you feeling afraid to meet your goals? Try to think of ways to overcome these fears. List ideas in your journal.

# Your Values

Try to figure out what you value most: honesty, courage, independence? As for me, I believe in all those things but especially being independent. I treasure my freedom to think and do as I please (within reason)—otherwise I'd go nuts!

You can write about your values in your journal. It's one way to understand what really matters to you. It's also a way to help you stick to your values.

Here's how to write about them: Make "I believe/ I don't believe" lists. Just draw a line down the middle of the page and fill in each column. Or, if you're not sure exactly what you believe in, try this:

* Think of the values that you have learned from your parents, teachers, friends, books, TV, etc., and list them in your journal.

* Read through the values and circle the ones you agree with. Write about why you believe in these things.

* Think about the things you didn't circle. Why don't you believe in them?

* Now that you know what you value, stand up for your beliefs. If anyone says your values are foolish, you can put that comment on your list of things you *don't* believe in!

| I *Believe:* | I *Don't Believe:* |
|---|---|
| *in equality for all people.* | *in censorship.* |
| *in not letting anyone or anything crush your love of learning, your creativity, or your curiosity.* | *in people forcing their own views on you.* |
| | *that school or parents are all bad, or all good.* |
| *that Girls are grrreat!* | *that I should have to wait till I'm 16 to drive or 18 to vote.* |
| *that teenagers are important.* | |
| *that everyone's ideas and views are worth listening to at least once (who knows what you might discover?).* | *that we can treat the earth however we want.* |
| *that we need to respect the earth.* | |
| *in freedom!* | |

# Wishes

You know how when you blow out the candles on your birthday cake, you're supposed to make a wish? Well, here's a way to change that tradition a little.

In your journal, write down as many wishes as the number of birthdays you've had (if you're 14, you get 14 wishes). What do you wish for? Your wishes can be big or small—just be sure not to tell anyone what they are!

## I wish

1. To remember a good joke.
2. For world peace . . . .

# Your Story

Your journal can be a great source of story ideas. Write down your every thought, impression, or inspiration. Keep notes about your feelings, your dreams, the weather—anything! Then, every so often, gather your past journals and read through the pages. Do the words inspire a story, a poem?

Use your past writings as ideas for a book or article about yourself (illustrate it, too). Even if you don't want to put yourself in the story, you can still use words from your journal to create a fictional place, a main character, and dialogue.

Many famous women writers used their girlhood journals to help them with books they wrote as adults. For example, L. M. Montgomery used her journals to help her create the characters of Anne and Emily, although by the time she actually wrote her books, she had burned the journal she kept from ages 9 to 13 (she regretted it, by the way). Also, Louisa May Alcott used her childhood journals to help her write *Little Women*. Most of the things she wrote about had really happened in her family.

It's important to write in your journal and to keep it for the future (don't burn it!). After all, one day you might have a great story to tell.

# Dreams

Dream interpretation may seem like something strange and mysterious that only mystics or scientists know about. That is absolutely not true! Anybody who wants to can interpret their dreams.

All you really need to do is write down your dreams as soon as you wake up. You can keep a journal or little notebook next to your bed just for that purpose.

Later in the day, you can read what you wrote and think about the dream. To figure out its meaning, think about what's going on in your life at the present time. What issues, events, or problems have come up?

For example, I once had a dream that I wrote a novel about the history of my hometown. I figured out what it might have meant. At the time, I was really hating my town and I think the dream was telling me to snap out of it. The message was: "Get over it! You live here so try to make the best of it." Now, I have to be honest: Sometimes I still don't like my hometown but not NEARLY as often.

By recording my dreams I can figure out what's on my mind. Use your Dream Journal to write or draw what your dream says to you. It's easy!

One last thing: If you're having a disturbing dream regularly, try this trick. Think about the dream (even write it down), then tell the dream that you don't believe in it. It might make the dream go away. I used to continually dream that a wolf was chasing my dad and me—I tried the trick and it worked for me, so it might work for you, too.

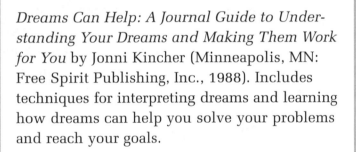

CHECK IT OUT

*Dreams Can Help: A Journal Guide to Understanding Your Dreams and Making Them Work for You* by Jonni Kincher (Minneapolis, MN: Free Spirit Publishing, Inc., 1988). Includes techniques for interpreting dreams and learning how dreams can help you solve your problems and reach your goals.

*The Secret Language of Dreams* by David Fontana (San Francisco, CA: Chronicle Books, 1994). This book has all sorts of dream symbols and what they might possibly mean in your dreams.

# What You Love to Do

Write about what you love to do. Is it sports, art, hanging out with your family, spending time with friends, riding your bike? How often do you do this hobby or activity?

Make your hobby a part of your journaling time. If you like to cook, you could copy recipes in your journal or make up new ones. If you like to sew, you could design clothes in your journal.

If you like to read, keep lists of books you've read or want to read, write book reviews, and copy favorite passages from your best-loved books. If you like art, your journal could contain your own art and reproductions of famous paintings (the same goes for photography).

No matter what your passion is (poetry, science, dance, animals), find a way to work it into your journal. It's your private place to dream of what you want to do and be.

# Love Yourself

Do you love yourself? (Be honest!) Liking who you are is essential. Many studies have proven that the healthier people are the ones who have good self-esteem.

If you don't love yourself, then write down why. Try learning to like yourself better (sometimes it's hard if people are teasing you, you're not doing very well in school, or you're comparing yourself to impossible standards—but it's still important).

Right now, think about your good qualities and NOT your bad ones. In your journal, write down ten (or more) things you love about you. If you can't think of ten, ask a friend or parent to name some of your good qualities. You may be surprised at what they have to say.

"*Delicious autumn!*
*My very soul is wedded to it.*"

Author George Eliot, from her letters

# Fall Journaling

This section is all about journaling activities that are fun for fall. You can try some or all of the following ideas or adapt them any way that works for you.

I love autumn because it's the time for jumping in piles of leaves, eating pumpkin pie, watching the leaves change color, and putting on your jacket in the evening to stare at the stars. It's also the time for going back to school. Although you may feel too busy with classes, after-school activities, and your friends, try to write in your journal as often as possible.

## Fall Journal Supplies

- A pencil
- A pen of desired color (preferably orange, brown, or red)
- Markers, crayons, paints, or colored pencils
- Camera and film
- Leaves to press
- Whatever else you want!

# Journaling Ideas

⋆ Write a poem about fall. To make your poem more detailed or lively, try to write about how the wind feels, sounds the leaves make, or the colors of autumn.

⋆ Using your colorful pen, write about why you like fall (or don't like it).

⋆ Describe what autumn means to you. (For example, is there a fall memory that stands out? How do you feel when autumn is coming?)

* Write a poem or story with a fall theme (apple cider, back to school, raking leaves, bonfires, pumpkins).

* Create a letter poem, using the letters of the word "fall" as the starting point of each line:

  **F**

  **A**

  **L**

  **L**

* For a variation on the letter poem, try using the words "Autumn" or "Leaves."

* Make a list of 5–10 words that describe fall.

* Write a ghost story. (I love them! They are especially delicious when you tell them around a campfire while roasting marsh-mallows, hot dogs, and bread twists.) Here are some ideas: a spooky legend, a disgusting horror story, a psychological thriller, a witch or vampire story. Don't forget to describe noises, feelings, scenery, or possibly add a surprise ending.

# From My Journal

*October 31, 1995 (Tuesday)*

*Dear Alison,*

*HAPPY HALLOWEEN! Today (after school anyway) was the perfect day. My neighborhood had their special trick-or-treating today! And it was from 5 to 7 P.M. when it was dark. The fact that it was raining didn't spoil it any. It made it better. It was so beautiful and eerie to be tromping through the streets, asking for candy and huddling against the cold, while the rain fell, the wind howled through the trees, and the jack-o'-lanterns grinned their ghoulish grins! I felt that I was racing with the night—I felt so free! I would like to always feel that way.*

*Love,*
*Jessica*

# Holiday Fun

* Draw a spooky Halloween picture or a Thanksgiving picture. Or sketch your dream Halloween costume.

* Certain foods are perfect in fall. Try the following recipe for an evening when you're sitting around a campfire with your family, telling stories and singing:

## Campfire Stew

### Ingredients:
- Chopped onions, carrots, and new potatoes
- Cut-up meat such as beef or pork (optional)
- Seasonings (salt, pepper, rosemary, basil, oregano, or anything you like)

### What to do:
Wrap all ingredients tightly in tin foil and place on glowing coals, turning the stew every so often, until it's thoroughly cooked. This will take about 20 minutes but test it to see if the ingredients are cooked through. Follow with s'mores (chocolate and marshmallows melted between graham crackers—yum!).

* Paint or draw an autumn scene. Or you can press some brightly colored leaves between the pages of your journal.

* Find a friend to take some photos with. Take pictures of yourselves wearing your Halloween costumes or playing in the leaves. Put the pictures in your journal, along with photos from your family's Thanksgiving dinner.

* Write about the people you want to spend Thanksgiving with and what you would like to eat at Thanksgiving dinner. Make a list of things you're thankful for.

## CHECK IT OUT

*Exploring Autumn* by Sandra Markle (NY: Avon, 1993). The author includes many things you can do outside and inside, plus autumn facts.

*Nicky the Nature Detective* by Ulf Svedberg, illustrated by Lena Anderson (NY: Farrar, Straus & Giroux, Inc., 1988). Nicky explores the beauty of fall and shows how a spider spins its web.

# Autumn Adventure

If you're looking for some story ideas for your journal, you can use the following story starter I wrote.

*Once upon a time there was a young woman and her name was* (fill in any name you like). *It was a sunny autumn day, so she decided to get up and go to her garden. She slipped into her sweatpants and went outside. She sat on her wicker bench and looked up into the trees, which were aflame with brightly colored leaves, and watched the squirrels busily collecting their winter food. The young woman thought she saw one squirrel with something shiny in its mouth, so she decided to follow it.*

*As she crept up closer to the squirrel, she could see what it was burying. A golden key! After the squirrel finished burying the key, the young woman went to dig it up.*

*"Well," she thought, "I have successfully found the key, but now where is the lock it fits in?"*

*"Most of the basic material a writer works with is acquired by the age of 15."*

Author Willa Cather

# Ideas for Your Journal

You can write about anything in your journal. Many journal-keepers simply write about what has happened to them that day. Other writers use the pages of their journal for poetry, song lyrics, stories, or thoughts about life.

If you can't think of anything to write, you might be experiencing writer's block. Don't worry, every writer goes through this at times. This section has journaling ideas for moving beyond writer's block (they are also fun to try anytime). You can use them in order or skip around until you find a suggestion that fits your mood.

# Free-Writing

Free-writing is a fun and easy activity to do in your journal. This exercise is also known as "stream-of-consciousness" writing. All you do is write whatever comes to mind—just let the words flow onto the paper.

When you free-write, don't worry about punctuation, spelling, or the quality of what you write. Simply write. Write until there's no more space on the page and without lifting your pen.

If you get stuck and can't think of anything, simply write "I'm stuck" until something comes to mind. Ready? Start now.

# Writing with Your Opposite Hand

A fun activity to try is writing with the hand you don't usually write with. (Don't worry about how bad the writing might look.) Do a whole journal entry this way, if possible. Because it's challenging to write with your opposite hand, you'll probably find that you write simpler sentences. You might even *think* differently as you write.

# Dialoguing

It's fun and easy to "talk" in your journal. Make up a dialogue or conversation that you would like to have with anyone—a famous person (alive or dead), your teacher, your hamster, a boy you like, etc.

Write the conversation as if you were writing dialogue in a play. You get to act as every speaker, figuring out what each person might have to say. Just write the name of the speaker, followed by a colon and the dialogue. Here's an example of one I did between me and my favorite author L. M. Montgomery:

**LMM:** *I hear you are one of my biggest fans.*

**Me:** *Yes, definitely. Even though your books were written long ago, they're so easy to relate to. I think every girl has a little of Anne of Green Gables in her!*

**LMM:** *That's why I wrote about Anne.*

**Me:** *I want to be a writer when I grow up. Do you have any tips for me?*

**LMM:** *All I have to say is write from your heart. Write what you need to write, not what someone else tells you to write.*

**Me:** *Thanks, I'll remember that!*

# My Day

What did you do today? Whether your day was really exciting or just plain dull, write about it in your journal. Try to capture details (the color of the sky, the smell of the hallways at school, what a friend said to you, the food you ate for dinner, your mood, and so on).

# Memories

Try to recall your best memory. Why is it your favorite? How about your worst memory? Your most embarrassing moment?

Relive these times in your journal. When you're writing, think about how you felt while the event was happening. Describe those feelings and how you feel now.

# Journals Are...

What does your journal mean to you? Write down your own definition, thoughts, and ideas. If you want, you can even write a poem about journaling (like the one I did below).

*Journals are places to keep*
*your most private thoughts.*
*They are your best friend when you are sad.*
*Journals know of every battle you've ever fought.*
*They are good places to go when you are glad.*
*Journals keep track of your thoughts and dreams.*
*They know your every goal.*
*Journals know how the world seems*
*when the universe takes its toll.*
*Journals are places to get a grip in.*
*They help you to climb mountains.*
*Journals are a cool well to dip in—*
*they're never-ending fountains.*

# Observer (Spy?)

Have you ever read the novel *Harriet the Spy?* Harriet is a girl who writes in her private notebook about everything—family, friends, school, love, life, the weather. Because she wants to be a writer when she grows up, she spies on people, secretly writing down their stories in her notebook.

Like Harriet, I carry a notebook around with me. I write down my thoughts about anything (people, school, computers, journaling, etc.). Later I expand on things in my journal. While I'm not saying you should spy on people's private lives, it's okay to be an observer. Watch what people do and listen to what they say, observe the scenery and the weather, and write down everything you hear and see.

## CHECK IT OUT

*Harriet the Spy* by Louise Fitzhugh (NY: Bantam Doubleday Dell Books, 1979). A wonderful story about a gutsy girl who loves to spy on the world and to write.

# World's Easiest Journal Entry

Here's the world's easiest journal entry. Just complete the following sentences in your journal:

* My name is...
* I was born on...
* I have (color? length? style?) hair...
* My teeth look like...
* I have (color?) eyes...
* My height is...
* In my family, I am the (oldest? youngest? middle child? only child?)...
* Names of my brothers and/or sisters...
* I have these kinds of pets (include their names, too)...
* My best friends are named...
* My favorite (book, song, food) is...
* I go to school at...
* I'm in this grade...
* My after-school activities are...
* On school nights I stay up until...
* On the weekend I stay up (sleep in?) until....

# Journal Review

Every once in a while, it's helpful to ask yourself how your journal writing is going. Do you enjoy it?

Think of ways to make journal-keeping more fun (get a new pen or some stickers?). If you write your journal entries on a computer, try playing around with different fonts.

Also think about whether you're journaling at the right time of day (or night) for you. Have you found the right place for your journal writing?

Whether you're still in love with journaling or running out of ideas, there are many books that can inspire you to pick up your pen. Read the diaries of a few famous women writers or look for books about keeping a journal.

# CHECK IT OUT

*The Diary of Latoya Hunter: My First Year in Junior High* by Latoya Hunter (NY: Vintage Books, 1994). Latoya, originally from Jamaica, was 12 when she began keeping a diary of her life in the Bronx. She shares her thoughts about school, parents, crushes, her Jamaican heritage, and inner-city life.

*Keeping Secrets: The Girlhood Diaries of Seven Women Writers* by Mary E. Lyons (NY: Henry Holt & Company, Inc., 1995). Includes Louisa May Alcott, Ida B. Wells, Charlotte Perkins Gilman, and others. Read about their personal journaling experiences.

*The Selected Journals of L. M. Montgomery,* edited by Mary Rubio and Elizabeth Waterston (Toronto: Oxford University Press, 1985). Lucy Maud Montgomery (my all-time favorite author) wrote the "Anne of Green Gables" books. You can probably find her journals, which are in three volumes, at your local library.

# Time Travel

Imagine what your life would be like if you had been born in another time and place. Who would you be? What would your typical day be like?

For example, how would your house and family look if you were born in France during the 1700s? Describe what it would have been like to be a queen in ancient Egypt. Imagine how you would survive each day if you were living during prehistoric times. Let your imagination run wild!

# Disguised Writing

Here's a way to make sure no one can read your private journal entry: Develop a secret code and write in it. Your code could be like hieroglyphics or a rebus, for example. For fun, you can also write your journal entry backwards. Hold the page up to the mirror to read it. Or try writing in invisible ink—on the next page is an easy recipe.

## Invisible Ink

### Ingredients:
Milk or grapefruit juice

### What to do:
Dip a toothpick or a dried felt-tip pen into the milk or grapefruit juice. Write your message and let it dry (you won't see your message). When you want to read it, hold the paper under a lightbulb or over a heated toaster and watch your message appear. You could also iron the paper lightly to see what you wrote.

# Boys!

Being a girl, you probably think about boys sometimes (ooh la la!). Write about any boys you like. Why do you like them? What do you wish they would say to you? If you don't like any boys at the present time, don't feel bad (I know how weird they can be).

## CHECK IT OUT

*What's Happening to My Body? Book for Boys: A Growing Up Guide for Parents and Sons* by Lynda Madaras (NY: Newmarket Press, 1988). Tells about the physical and emotional changes that happen to boys during puberty. Maybe it will help you understand them better (yeah, right).

# Dear Reader

*If you are between the ages of 11 and 16, you're probably going through some changes, both physical and mental, as I am. So I decided to add this special section that's all about growing up.*

*The next section provides information about physical changes you're going through and things that might be on your mind. There are also journaling activities and a list of recommended resources that tells you where to go to find more answers. I hope that as you read this, you'll realize you're not alone. Each girl may look different on the outside, but in many ways we are the same on the inside. We all face the struggles of growing up and need to be accepted and loved for who we are.*

*Love,*
*Jessica*

*P.S. Remember, billions of girls before you have survived puberty and you can, too.*

*"I think that what's happening to me is so wonderful, and I don't just mean the changes taking place on the outside of my body, but also those on the inside."*

Anne Frank, from her diary

# Growing Up

Your body is probably growing and changing
in a lot of ways right now (I know mine is).
Don't worry about it too much.

Or, if you don't seem to be growing and
changing as fast as your friends are, don't
worry about that either. Each of us goes at
our own pace. Be comfortable with how
you look and who you are!

# Your Height

You may feel too short or too tall, but I have good news for you. For those of you who feel like King Kong compared to other girls, you'll probably stop growing sooner than everyone else, and then people will start catching up to you. For those who feel like Thumbelina compared to others, you're just growing a little more slowly—soon you'll probably start catching up. If you're still concerned, this chart shows the average heights of girls of different ages.

| Age | 10 | 11 | 12 | 13 | 14 | 16 | 18 |
|---|---|---|---|---|---|---|---|
| Avg. Height | 4'6" | 4'9" | 4'11" | 5'2" | 5'3" | 5'4" | 5'4" |
| Height Range (90% of girls) | 4'2" to 4'11" | 4'4" to 5'2" | 4'6" to 5'5" | 4'9" to 5'7" | 4'10" to 5'8" | 5'0" to 5'8" | 5'0" to 5'9" |

**Note:** Don't be concerned if you're average, above average, or below average. There's nothing wrong with being tall, short, or right in the middle.

# Your Appearance

Many girls worry too much about their looks during the teen years. Take good care of yourself but don't get obsessed with your appearance.

At this time in your life, you're probably noticing changes in your body and your face. For example, you may start noticing pimples, whiteheads, and blackheads. They are a natural part of growing up, and almost everybody is affected by them during puberty. Wash your face each morning and night to keep it clean. Never squeeze or pick at zits because they will probably flare up even more. For more serious cases, you may need to see a dermatologist.

Body hair is another thing you're probably noticing. It's a bother, isn't it? Pubic, leg, and underarm hair usually starts developing when you're anywhere from 9 to 14. For instance, I'm 14 and I started shaving my legs when I was 12. I didn't start shaving my pits until this summer. (By the way, some girls and women never shave and that's okay, too.) I tweeze my eyebrows because otherwise it looks as though I only have one eyebrow. As for pubic hair, well that's another story....

# Your Weight

In many polls asking girls what they'd like to change about themselves, half say they would change their weight. Does that mean that a lot of girls are too fat or too skinny? NO! They simply compare themselves to the impossible standards that the media gives us—teeny waists and large breasts.

Here is a quick quiz: Do you think you're too fat? Do you go on crash diets? Do you skip meals as a way of dieting? If your answer to one or more of these questions is yes, you might have an eating disorder.

Anorexia and bulimia are eating disorders. An anorexic usually eats very little and exercises strenuously. She may starve herself till she's only skin and bones, but when she looks in the mirror she thinks she's fat. Anorexia can lead to heart ailments, loss of periods, bone damage, and other serious problems, and it can be fatal in up to 10 percent of all cases.

A bulimic usually eats heavily, then takes laxatives or diuretics, or sticks her finger down her throat to make herself vomit. Bulimics are also prone to over-exercising, but unlike anorexics they are usually of average weight or overweight. Bulimia can lead to dental, stomach, bowel, heart, and circulatory disorders and may even cause early death.

There are clinics that offer medical and counseling help for bulimics and anorexics. Many of the clinics use journals as part of the recovery process, so patients can write and draw about their feelings, experiences, and progress. If you or anyone you know has an eating disorder, please get help right away. Talk to an adult you trust and do it today!

## CHECK IT OUT

If you or a friend needs help with an eating disorder, or if you're looking for information, you can call the American Anorexia/Bulimia Association in New York (212) 501-8351. They are available Monday through Friday, from 9 A.M. to 5 P.M. EST to answer your questions, send some reading materials, or refer you to a local counselor for more help.

# Your Period

Hearing about menstruation and the other changes of puberty may scare you, but these changes don't all happen overnight. You'll have plenty of time to get comfortable with them.

During puberty, girls start menstruating, or getting their period. The menstrual fluid that leaves your body is bloody but painless (although some girls may experience cramps, backaches, etc.). During your period, you'll use pads or tampons for protection.

Despite anything you may have heard otherwise, you can swim, play sports, or take a shower while having your period—you can do anything you would normally do. Grown women usually get their period once a month, but girls who are just starting to menstruate may get it more or less often than this.

Before your period, you may experience Premenstrual Syndrome (PMS). This is a medical condition that affects girls and women in various ways and can produce a lot of physical and psychological symptoms.

The symptoms, ranging from mild to severe, usually begin two weeks before menstruation. Main physical symptoms include bloating, weight gain, breast pain, backache, cramps, pimples, and a craving for sweets. Feelings of tension and depression and difficulty sleeping are some of the common psychological problems.

The causes of PMS are commonly believed to be hormones, body chemistry, and nutrition. Treatment for the condition includes eating foods high in protein and minerals and very low in salt, avoiding caffeine and alcohol, and exercising regularly. In more severe cases, hormones, tranquilizers, and other prescription drugs may be used. If you have very uncomfortable PMS or periods, talk to your doctor.

# Coming-of-Age Ceremony

Many cultures have traditionally celebrated the time when a girl gets her first period. You can, too, by having a coming-of-age ceremony. This is a way to help yourself, your friends, and your family to realize that the female body isn't something to be ashamed of—it should be cherished and celebrated. Getting your period is part of the magic of being a girl.

When you have your ceremony, you can do anything you want. You might choose to have a party with your female friends and relatives, go out and buy yourself something special, or just have a small celebration by yourself in your room. You might wear a special outfit or choose certain music to listen to. (Don't forget to write about it in your journal.)

# Journaling Ideas

* Write about your ideal coming-of-age ceremony.

* Describe how you felt when you got your first period (glad? not so glad?).

* Make a list of ten things you love about your body.

# From My Journal

*November 13, 1994 (Sunday)*

*Dear Victoria,*

*Today I got my first period. I know that I was ranting and raving about not having it before, but now that I have it I am not so sure that I want it!! But oh well, it will be all right. At least I can have a coming-of-age ceremony. And happy early thirteenth birthday to me! I have to go now.*

*Love,*
*Jessica*

# Your Changing Body

You are probably aware of this, but your breasts may begin developing when you're between the ages of 9 and 14. If you think that you are way behind or ahead of other girls, hang in there. Many girls worry about breast size but shouldn't. (I know it's hard not to worry when TV shows, movies, and magazine ads seem to focus so much on big breasts.)

Another change you may notice is a small amount of a clear or milky white fluid, or discharge, from the walls of the vagina that may leave a slight yellow stain on your underwear. The fluid is called vaginal discharge, which is a completely normal sign that your body is maturing. This fluid helps to keep your vagina clean and healthy. Many girls notice this discharge a year or two before their first period. Others don't notice it until they've started menstruating, and some don't have it at all. If you see a brownish or reddish color in it (spotting), this may signal that your period is soon to come (lucky you!?).

Okay, we can't ignore this one: masturbation. Masturbation is rubbing or touching the genitals in a way that feels good. There are many harmful myths about masturbation, none of which are true. You may have heard that only boys masturbate.

You may have been told that if you masturbate it will keep you from enjoying sexual intercourse later in life. You may have heard that it makes you blind. None of these are true! Masturbating does not hurt you. It's normal if you masturbate, and it's also normal if you don't.

# The "S" Word (Sex)

At this time in your life, you're probably starting to have thoughts about sex. The best rule to go by is: Don't compromise yourself by doing something you're not ready for. Your body should be sacred to you, so treat it with the respect it deserves. Following are 10 of what I think are the worst reasons to have sex:

1. Your boyfriend is threatening to break up with you if you don't. (This just proves he doesn't truly love or respect you.)

2. Your boyfriend begs you so often that you think you should just give in. (He's acting like a child, which shows he's not as ready as he thinks.)

3. Your friends are talking about sex, and you feel left out of the conversation. (Try changing the subject.)

4. You don't like being called a virgin. (What's so bad about that word anyway? I think it's nice.)

5. Your boyfriend says his ex-girlfriend always had sex with him, so you should, too. (Maybe he should have stayed with her then?)

6. Having sex will prove you're in love. (If you are truly in love, you can wait till the time is right.)

7. Your friends say they have sex so you should, too. (Are these people really your friends? Try to find friends who are more supportive. Also remember that lots of people brag about having sex when it really isn't true.)

8. You will feel more grown-up. (Don't be in such a hurry to grow up—you'll probably have to be an adult for about 50 or 60 years, so why rush things?)

9. You're feeling rebellious. (There are better ways to rebel—start a band, become an activist....)

10. You want to feel loved and needed. (You *are* loved. You *are* needed. Enjoy the love of your family and friends. Love yourself.)

And here is what I think is the best reason to have sex: You are totally ready for it. This means you can answer yes to all of these questions:

* Are you mature enough to handle the strong feelings and responsibilities?

* Are you in a committed relationship with someone who is mature enough to handle the strong feelings and responsibilities? (In my opinion, being married is best.)

* Do you know about sexually transmitted diseases (STDs)? Do you know how to protect yourself from STDs? Is your partner someone you can trust 100 percent?

* Do you respect yourself? Do you respect your partner? Does your partner respect you?

* Do you know about birth control? Are you ready to use birth control if you don't want to get pregnant right away?

* If you do want to get pregnant right away, are you ready to spend the next 18 years of your life taking care of another human being? Is your partner ready? Do you have the financial resources?

* Is having sex what YOU really, really want, or would you rather wait?

# CHECK IT OUT

*Changing Bodies, Changing Lives: A Book for Teens on Sex and Relationships* by Ruth Bell (NY: Random House, Inc., 1988). This book has a lot of information about the physical and mental changes of growing up. My favorite parts are the brief section on keeping a diary and the quotes and poetry about growing up—all by people our age!

*I'm On My Way Running: Women Speak On Coming of Age,* edited by Lyn Reese, Jean Wilkinson, and Phyllis S. Koppelman (NY: Avon, 1995). Lovely, goose-bump wonderful stories and poems that connect you with adolescent girls from the past and present.

*The Information Please Girls' Almanac* by Alice Siegel and Margo McLoone (Boston, MA: Houghton Mifflin Company, 1995). Discusses what happens to your body during puberty and ways to take care of your body. There's a calendar of women's words, birthdays, events, firsts, and more.

*My Body, My Self for Girls: The "What's Happening to My Body?" Workbook* by Lynda Madaras (NY: Newmarket Press, 1993). A workbook all about the physical changes in your body.

*My Feelings, My Self: Lynda Madaras' Growing-Up Guide for Girls* by Lynda Madaras (NY: Newmarket Press, 1993). A workbook all about the emotional changes of growing up.

*Our Bodies, Ourselves: A Book by and for Women, 25th Anniversary Edition* by the Boston Women's Health Book Collective Staff (NY: Simon & Schuster, 1996). Features some of the most up-to-date information you can find on women's bodies, health, and feelings.

*What's Happening to My Body? Book for Girls: A Growing Up Guide for Parents and Daughters* by Lynda Madaras (NY: Newmarket Press, 1987). A fact-packed book (complete with diagrams) about the physical and emotional changes you're going through.

*"The process of writing,
any form of creativity,
is a power intensifying life."*

Rita Mae Brown in *Starting from Scratch*

# Journaling Activities

Are you ready to get even more creative with your journaling? There are lots of fun art and writing activities you can do.

You can personalize your journal with artwork, write something special on your birthday, and even use your journal as a way to start your own newsletter or zine. This section has ideas for times when you're looking to try something a little different.

# Journal Cover

You can design your very own journal cover. Draw pictures of things you like, yourself, people you know, or anything else that has to do with you. You can even draw fantasy objects, like unicorns or other mythical creatures—be creative.

If you don't want to draw, try a collage. Cut out pictures from magazines and catalogs and paste them on the cover of your journal. Use glitter glue or paint to add more color.

Write anything you like on the cover, such as "My Journal" or "Private!" Try calligraphy or fancy writing. Whatever you do, let the real you come through.

*The Beezus and Ramona Diary* by Beverly Cleary (NY: William Morrow & Company, Inc., 1986). A fill-in journal for girls. It has fun ideas, pictures, and quotes.

*The Creative Journal: The Art of Finding Yourself* by Lucia Capacchione, Ph.D. (North Hollywood, CA: Newcastle Publishing Company, Inc., 1989). This book has creative ideas for teens and adults.

*The Creative Journal for Teens: Making Friends with Yourself* by Lucia Capacchione, Ph.D. (North Hollywood, CA: Newcastle Publishing Company, Inc., 1992). A book for teens, with all sorts of self-discovery activities.

*Pages and Pockets: A Portfolio for Secrets and Stuff,* illustrated by Merle Nacht (Middleton, WI: Pleasant Company Publications, 1995). Another illustrated fill-in journal with lots of creative ideas.

# Journal Companion

Do you want someone (or something) to keep you company while you're journaling? Then make your very own journal companion. Here's how:

* Find paper, a pencil or pen, scissors, and markers or crayons.

* Draw a person or creature, color it, cut it out, and give it a name.

* Keep your new companion inside your journal.

# Comic Strip

Create your own comic strip in your journal. You can be the main character (even a superhero) or just make one up. The strip can be one panel or a series of panels. This activity can be a way to practice your cartooning, to experiment with humor, or even to explore your feelings.

Or you can collect funny comic strips from the Sunday edition of your newspaper and paste them in your journal. You can read them whenever you need a laugh or a little inspiration.

# Trading Cards

If you like trading cards, here's a fun way to make your own. All you need are unlined index cards and a pencil or pen. (It's more fun if you also use markers, colored pencils, watercolors, photos, and glue.)

For your very own personalized trading cards, write your "life story" or "vital statistics" on one side of the index card. For example, you can put your height, hair color, eye color, likes and dislikes, favorite school subjects, best-loved book, etc.

It's also fun to add inspiring quotes (your own or ones by famous people). On the other side of the card, do a self-portrait. You can draw or paint yourself or just glue a photo. Store your trading cards inside your journal or trade them with friends.

# On Your Birthday

A great birthday journal activity is to write a letter to the "old you" (meaning the age you were before the birthday) and another letter to the "new you" (who you are now and who you want to be for the whole next year).

Every year on my birthday, I do this. I describe the good and bad things about the age of the "old me." For the "new me" letter, I write down wishes and ask myself some questions.

Then on my next birthday, I reread the birthday letters from the previous year to see if I can now answer the old questions and to see if any of my wishes came true. I also write two new letters.

Another idea: Celebrate your birthday in your journal. Find out what national events happened on the day you were born (visit your school or local library to do the research). It's fun to read headlines from local or national newspapers that came out on your birthday (you can find your local paper, and usually the *New York Times,* on microfilm). Photocopy the front pages of popular magazines from the day you were born and paste the pages in your journal.

# Journal Newsletter

You can make your own special newsletter about journal-keeping. First, write some articles on journaling (what to write, things to draw, why journal-keeping is important, etc.). You can also write a book review about a book on journaling (maybe even this book?).

Next, edit the articles by trying to fix any grammar, spelling, or punctuation mistakes. Change words around or do whatever you want to polish the articles. After that, type them up.

On the final version, add some fun cartoons, jokes, or riddles. Illustrate your newsletter with computer graphics, drawings, rubber stamps, and stickers.

Try to give your newsletter a fun title. Last but not least, make copies for your readers (friends and family).

# Journal Zine

It's fun to start your own zine and a good place to try it is in your journal. I used to write a lot of different zines. I created *Hey World, Here I Am!* for myself and *Scrapbook* for my younger cousins. My friend Alison and I had a zine called *Ladybug* that was private just between us. Now I write *Chocolate Pizza* for any girl who wants to read it.

Create a zine starring you. Include your photo, your likes and dislikes, your opinions, your secrets—anything. Once you get the hang of it, try publishing your zine for family and friends to read. Here are some suggestions for making your own zine*:

> If you want to start your own zine, I suggest making it about yourself—it's a subject you know a lot about, and when you dish the dirt on your inner thoughts, I guarantee people will read. Not ready for that kind of exposure? Pick a topic you know and love—collecting PEZ dispensers, speaking Klingon, working behind the counter at Dunkin' Donuts.
>
> Once you've decided on a topic, you'll need to figure out how much time and money you want

---

* Excerpted with permission from "Behind the Zines" by Pagan Kennedy, *seventeen* (March 1995): pages 142, 149.

to sink into producing your zine. With access to a computer, desktop publishing software like Aldus PageMaker or Quark XPress, a scanner, and a laser printer, you could put out something as real-worldly as *seventeen.* That kind of setup costs big bucks, and I'm by no means saying run out and buy this stuff. If your school has a swinging computer room, use that equipment for free or rent time on equipment at a computer center. Of course, making a fancy zine with fancy software can cause fancy problems. You may spend a lot of time asking yourself questions like, "Why can't I get this text to wrap around that graphic?" when you'd rather be asking yourself questions like, "How can I use this zine as an excuse to meet local rock stars?" I suggest you play with the programs, get some proficiency, and *then* start laying out your opus.

If you don't want to deal with (or can't get your hands on) Aldus or Quark, there's always Plan B. Get yourself access to a decent computer (like a 386 if you're in IBM-compatible land, or just about any Mac) and use a sophisticated word-processing package like Microsoft Word, WordPerfect, or Word for Windows. These packages will let you do a lot of cool things—use computer clip art (a file of cheesy but useful pictures), put text in boxes, print in columns. Can't scare up even this kind of technology? Then try Plan C. That's C as in cheap—and my preferred plan. If you're not afraid to produce a less slick zine, then all you need is a typewriter. You'll be putting this zine together by hand, so listen up. Go to the art store and buy some layout grid boards. Using the grids to make sure everything's straight, lay down the headlines, strips of text, and pictures with rubber cement. To spice up the design, I like to use rub-on letters or clip-art "decorative alphabets." The wackiest typeface I've ever seen, called Daisyland, looks like it should be on the cover of a Deee-Lite album....

When you're finished writing and illustrating and laying out, find a photocopier, run off copies, collate and staple them, and then distribute your zine to your friends....

# Story Group

You can start a Story Group to share reading and writing activities. The group can be made up of your friends who love to read and write. Here are some suggestions to get you started (but remember, there's plenty of room to explore—group members will probably have great ideas, too).

* Set regular meeting days and times (every two weeks works well).

* Choose a book for everyone to read before each meeting (each member can buy a copy or check the book out at the library). Discuss the book.

* Have everybody bring a journal (it doesn't have to be fancy—a cheap notebook will do). Then write your thoughts and impressions of the book. You can do this before or during each meeting.

* Think of other journal-writing projects (for example, a poem based on a character in the book or a new ending for the book).

* Share your writings and offer *constructive* criticism.

* Write letters to your favorite authors.

# Journal Group

Journal writers can become lifelong companions. If you have any friends who keep diaries or journals, you might want to start a Journal Group.

You can meet face-to-face at a certain time (weekly, monthly, etc.) to talk and write. Spend time sharing journal ideas or reading entries aloud, if you want. Or start a Journal Group online (I have had great success doing this!). It's a lot of fun, and the people are usually very supportive.

Privacy and respect are big issues with journal groups. If one member judges, criticizes, or makes rude remarks to another member, I suggest (this may sound harsh) that you boot her out of the group immediately! Journal groups are based on trust and what is said in the circle should go no further.

*Warning:* If someone in the group reveals that she is in danger in some way (for example, she has experienced abuse or is suicidal), this is a time to break the confidentiality rule and tell someone who can help. Ask an adult you trust. Don't wait.

# 3 Journal Group Rules

1. Anyone may share, but no one should be pressured to share something too private.

2. People treat each other with respect.

3. What is said in the group stays in the group.

# School's-Out Journal

Here's a fun way to get your friends into journaling. After the last day of school, invite your closest friends over for a school's-out party. Sure, have the traditional games, food, and videos, but there's more: The best part is what's in the goodie bags.

Make the goodie bags ahead of time (you can simply use brown paper bags and decorate them), and in each one put an unlined notebook. Or, to make a notebook, choose different colors of paper from an office supply store (you'll need about 50 pages for each book) and add a front and back cover made of heavier-stock paper. Many office supply stores have a special machine that can bind the pages together.

Decorate each notebook, using any art supplies you have on hand. You might want to write a title on each cover—something like "School's-Out Journal" or "Sisterhood Journal"—and add the name of the person you're giving it to. Then put some fun journaling supplies in each goodie bag (pencils, erasers, stickers, etc.). You can even add a list of journal-keeping tips to each package.

After you have handed out your goodie bags, ask everyone to write a special oath on the first page of their journals.

Here's an example:

> *"We all belong to the International
> Sisterhood of Women, we all have power
> and strong voices, and we're all friends.
> This summer, we vow to keep journals,
> writing down our innermost thoughts
> and feelings. Signed...."*

Each person can sign her name at the bottom
of each oath page. Then if you (or any of the others)
need inspiration, all you have to do is look at the
oath to feel connected. When everyone gets together
again (possibly on the day before school starts), you
can all have fun sharing your writings.

*"There is a privacy about [winter] which no other season gives you…. Only in the winter…can you have longer, quiet stretches when you can savor belonging to yourself."*

Ruth Stout in *How to Have a Green Thumb Without an Aching Back*

# Winter Journaling

I love the winter cold, when your breath makes clouds in the air. I wake up on winter mornings to find that Jack Frost has left a secret message on my window, or I gaze up at the night sky to look for ice crystals on the moon. Think of all the wonderful things you can do in the snow, such as build a snowman (snow-woman?) or make snow angels. (Or have you ever tried dripping a little red food coloring in the snow, then lying face down next to it so people think you're dead?)

Winter also brings holidays and good times with family and friends. Although it may be cold outside, I always feel warmer on the inside. Write all about winter in your journal—how it looks, the way it feels, and everything you do during the season.

## Winter Journal Supplies

- A pencil
- A pen of desired color (preferably red or green)
- Markers, crayons, paints, or colored pencils
- Glue and scissors
- Whimsical bits of fabric, glitter, stickers, sequins, etc.
- Cards, photos, and your memories!

# Journaling Ideas

⋆ What are your favorite winter memories? Think about times you shared with friends and family, sledding, making a snowman, etc.

⋆ Write a poem about winter (for example, what you like or don't like about the season, or what winter means to you).

⋆ List 10 words that describe snow. Or, if you live in a warmer climate, what are some signs of winter in your area?

* Describe your favorite winter vacation. Where would you go to get warm?

* Write a poem or story that has winter details (gingerbread cookies, pine trees, snow or snowflakes, shoveling, etc.).

* Write a children's story. For example, you could create a legend about the origin of winter.

## CHECK IT OUT

*Celia's Island Journal* by Celia Thaxter (NY: Little, Brown & Company, 1992). Read about Celia's dreary island winters and how she and her younger brother kept themselves busy.

*Christmas Journal* by Mary Engelbreit (Kansas City, MO: Andrews & McMeel, 1994). This journal has beautiful illustrations. You can fill in all your favorite holiday memories.

# From My Journal

*December 25, 1993 (Saturday)*

*Dear Diary,*

*Today is Christmas Day! I've had so much fun. We are about to have our big delicious dinner of Cornish game hen. Last night I got the Addy doll! She is so lovely! I love her.*

*I also got a teddy bear named Benjamin, two candy canes, and a gingerbread cookie from Mike and Jerry. We went to church and then came home and watched "The Muppet Christmas Carol."*

*I slept well until 5:30 A.M. when I wanted to get up, but my parents made me sleep until 7:00. I am glad. I guess parents do know best. SOMETIMES!*

*I am sitting in front of the fireplace, and it is so warm and cozy. I am playing a CD on my new CD player right now. The day after tomorrow we are going to Michigan. Yahoo!*

*My little cousin Kara got a Samantha doll for Christmas. I am happy for her. I know I will share many good times with Addy. I am taking her to Michigan.*

*I will NOT grow out of dolls, stuffed animals, or magic for a LONG time or ever. Well, I am going to go use one of the things I got for Christmas.*

*Love,*
*Jessica*

# Holiday Fun

* Draw or paint a winter nature scene. Or design a fancy holiday outfit for yourself.

* Make a fanciful holiday collage, using fabric, glitter, stickers, sequins, and any other items you can find.

* Make a scrapbook to collect your holiday photos, drawings, concert tickets, greeting cards, or any other fun stuff. Write a caption under each item, using red or green ink.

* Design a holiday greeting card for a friend. You can make it by hand or create one on a computer.

* In your journal, write your own Christmas or Hanukkah legend. Or write a story about your dream winter holiday.

* Add journaling items to your gift wish-list: pens, a new journal, art supplies, stickers, and so on.

* Put together a holiday gift list that includes presents you plan to give to your friends, family members, or a charity. Try to think of the "perfect" gift. Remember, the perfect gift isn't always the one that's the most expensive (try homemade cookies or any handmade present).

* Answer the following questions: What do I want most this holiday season? What is my best holiday memory ever? If I had magic powers, how would I use them this holiday season?

* Don't forget your New Year's resolutions (you know, those things you promise to do or not to do in the coming year). You can keep track of your resolutions in your journal (like I do) but try not to make more than three to five. Don't pick resolutions that are impossible to keep and don't feel guilty if you can't keep them. I usually resolve to try to write in my journal at least once a week.

* Remember, winter is also the season for Valentine's Day! (By the way, my personal feeling is that Valentine's Day is a crock. It just makes you feel guilty if you don't have a boyfriend or girlfriend, when you are perfectly perfect without one.) This year, give yourself a Valentine's Day gift—a book, a pen, a new journal, flowers, a stuffed animal, candy, even a card. Make it a day for celebrating you.

* Write a love letter to . . . yourself. What do you love about yourself? You can express it in a poem or on a Valentine's Day card meant for your eyes only.

# Advice for Life:

1. Love yourself.

2. Be yourself.

3. Always keep a journal.

# Different Kinds of Journals

You can have one journal or a dozen, depending on your preference. I have several journals but my main one is a three-ring binder. I write all my journal entries and record my dreams in it.

I have another binder that's my creative journal for drawing, sketching, and writing poems, story ideas, song lyrics, music, and special projects from journaling books. I keep a little notebook with me at all times to write down my thoughts and ideas. I also journal on my computer. Here are some suggestions for different kinds of journals you can try.

# Art Journal

Draw, sketch, paint, or doodle in your Art Journal. You can take this kind of journal and a pencil with you anyplace, and when you see something beautiful or meaningful to you, sketch it. (If you want, bring crayons, markers, colored pencils, watercolors, and a paintbrush.)

You might be thinking, "But I'm not an artist!" You don't have to be. Anyone can draw, paint, or doodle, and you don't have to show your work to other people if you don't want to.

You *can* draw, so give it a try. Just be sure to date your art and write a brief description of the scene that inspired you.

Here are some Art Journal ideas:

* Draw a make-believe country, complete with a map of its roads, mountains, lakes, and landmarks. Give the country a name.

* Design a cool outfit for yourself. You can even sketch yourself wearing it, complete with a new hairstyle and makeup.

* Paint your self-portrait or paint yourself as you think you'll look in 10 years. For fun, try doing the picture as a caricature.

* Make a collage using any materials at hand—tissue paper, cut-outs from magazines, dried leaves or flowers.

* Draw your dream house, inside and out.

* Make up a new planet. Draw or paint it.

# Computer Journal

You can journal right on your computer. I do this, but I still keep a hand-written journal so I can write anywhere—in the car, at school, in the woods, etc. If you journal on your computer, figure out how to "hide" or "lock" personal files and don't forget your password!

I use different computer programs to help me do creative writing projects and design stickers, posters, and comic strips. You can find all sorts of fun computer programs at your nearest software store. The programs will probably have lots of fun fonts, borders, clip art, and graphics to experiment with (my favorite fonts are Comic Sans MS, Lucida Calligraphy, and Courier New).

Another fun thing to try is creating your own Home Page. (You need a computer with a modem for this.) If you subscribe to an online service like Prodigy, find out about guidelines and templates for creating a Home Page.

Here are some ideas for your own Home Page:

* Post entries from your journal (if you don't mind others reading them) and include your life history and photos of yourself.

* Make your page catchy and colorful by adding graphics to the text. (If it's all text, it might seem a little dull. But don't add *too* many graphics because some readers might not have a fast modem.)

* Start an "E-zine." (It's like a zine, only it's on the World Wide Web.) Your E-zine can be about you, about life as a girl, or any subject you find interesting. You can bring out your E-zine as many times per year as you want. (My E-zine is called "Girl World.")

## CHECK IT OUT

This Web site has all sorts of information on setting up a Home Page—for free!

http://www.angelfire.com/freepages/index.html

# Friendship Journal

This kind of journal is for sharing with a friend. To keep a Friendship Journal, all you need is some kind of notebook (and a friend who wants to journal with you). If you want, you can decorate the cover. A Friendship Journal works for friends who live far away or right down the block.

In the journal, write about what's happening to you, memories of the things that you and your friend have done (or things you still do), and anything else that comes to mind. It's also fun to draw pictures, write little stories, and decorate the pages with stickers and rubber stamps. A Friendship Journal is a great way to show your creativity and keep in touch with a friend.

I have had a great experience using this type of journal. One of my best friends lives in Maryland, but we still keep in touch through journal-writing. We each started out with our own notebook, decorated it, and began writing. We kept up the journals for a month, then sent them to each other.

After reading each other's journals, we sent them back so we could continue writing in them. I have only one tip for this kind of journal: Try to write every day (even just a few sentences!). If that's not possible, try to write at least once a week. This way, your far-away friend gets more news about you.

If you share a Friendship Journal with someone who lives close by, try writing a "partner poem." For this project, you and your friend can sit outside with your journals (this can work indoors, too). Then each of you writes a few observations about your surroundings and several statements about yourself. Switch notebooks and read each other's writings. Each of you can then try composing a poem based on what the other has written.

For a little variety, you can try a journal that's tape-recorded or put on videotape. This way you can see and/or hear each other, and you can sing and tell jokes. A recorded journal may also take less time and postage. Added advantage: Other people can talk on it, too.

One last option for keeping a written Friendship Journal is to design it as one big, unsent letter. After you have been writing in it for a while (don't forget to date the entries), name the journal after your friend and give it to her. If you want, you can even type it up on your computer or typewriter.

# Scrapbook Journal

In the summer, I like to keep a Scrapbook Journal. (You can keep this kind of journal any time of year, but summer is a good season for it since you may have more free time.)

You can write and draw in your Scrapbook Journal, but it's also a great place to paste things that remind you of summer. All you need is a large blank or lined book (blank is best), pens, pencils, markers, crayons and/or colored pencils, glue or clear tape, and a camera and film.

Following is a list of suggestions for what to collect:

* concert programs
* cards, postcards, or letters from friends and relatives
* souvenir napkins or menus
* friends' autographs
* beach pebbles or sand
* feathers, pressed leaves, and/or wildflowers
* news clippings
* maps of family trips with routes highlighted

* reviews of movies you see or books
  you read
* party invitations
* photos of yourself and of your family
  and friends
* ticket stubs from movies, plays,
  or sporting events.

You can also write about your summer experiences (picnics, weirdest food eaten, your trip to the zoo, slumber parties, favorite ice-cream flavors, and so on). Try keeping a record of the following: sports scores of your favorite teams, hit songs, favorite books, money earned at a summer job, jokes and riddles you heard or told, and inches you grew.

A Scrapbook Journal is a fun place for art such as portraits, nature scenes, handprints, footprints, or thumbprints. Draw anything that catches your eye or captures your imagination—insects, flowers, cloud formations, even your daydreams!

# Family Journal

A Family Journal is one that your immediate family or your extended family shares. You can put anything in it: news, thoughts, feelings, announcements, memories, family mementos, etc.

It's great to share a journal with your extended family because it helps you feel closer to family members you might not see very often. A journal within your immediate family encourages communication and is a way to share memories.

To start your Family Journal, you can draw pictures or write about things that have happened to you or a family member, or funny family stories and legends. You might write trivia questions about your family history and see if people can come up with the right answers. Record things your family has done together (vacations, events, celebrations). If someone in your family has died, you can write your memories of that person and what he or she meant to you.

Then pass the journal on to the next person or family so others can write in it, too. Try sharing your Extended Family Journal using the round-robin system, where one family member or family keeps the journal for a certain amount of time before sending it to the next on the list (or you can share the journal at family reunions).

If it doesn't work for you to have this kind of Family Journal, you can still use your regular journal to record information about your family. One idea is to make a family tree. You'll need to find out the following information for each family member and relative:

    ✴ full name (list the last name first),

    ✴ date and place of birth,

    ✴ date and place of marriage,

    ✴ date and place of death.

You can get this information by interviewing your parents, grandparents, and other members of your family. If they don't live nearby, write a letter asking for the information you need or just give them a call. This is a fun way to get in touch with people you may not see too often. And some of your older relatives might really enjoy sharing their memories with you!

# Writer's Journal

A Writer's Journal is a great tool if you think you want to be a writer when you grow up. Use it to jot down story ideas, to record your impressions and descriptions of people, to capture a conversation on paper, and to simply write poems and stories.

You can also use this type of journal to keep track of your favorite passages from anything you read (books, poems, magazines, famous diaries, etc.). Next time you come across something wonderful—great dialogue, a vivid character or scene—save it. Simply write it down in your Writer's Journal to savor it later.

# From My Story
## "Phoebe"

Following is a passage from a story I wrote called "Phoebe." I got the descriptions of Washington, D.C., from the time I visited. I think it's the best big city in the world (besides Boston).

*I miss Grandma. No one else understands me so well. Today I went to the place Grandma and I used to go all the time. It's a little place in Farragut Square that we usually had all to ourselves. We would sit under what we called the "Sister Tree." The reason we called it that is because it looked like it had a picture of the twins Gemini carved into the bark—it was special because Grandma and I are both Geminis.*

*It's the most beautiful place in the whole park! The sunlight shines dappled through the tree branches, and the grass feels like soft velvet. And it smells so good! Like chocolate and cinnamon, mixed together in a perfect scent . . . .*

*"I believe that it is spring within me, I feel that spring is awakening, I feel it in my whole body and soul."*

Anne Frank, from her diary

# Spring Journaling

Spring is a time of new beginnings. Here are some surefire signs of spring: lots of people outside, warm breezes, a "foggy" sun, dogs barking, birds singing, buds on the trees and flowers, geese flying north, and the smell of hotdogs cooking on the grill.

Take advantage of the sunny, warm weather and fresh air by writing in your journal outdoors. Here are some ideas for saying hello to spring.

## Spring Journal Supplies

- Pencil or pen (green is preferable)
- Crayons, markers, paints, or colored pencils
- Scissors, glue, tape, stapler
- Camera and film
- Your mind, body, and imagination!

# Journaling Ideas

⋆ Write your own spring legend (how spring came to be or why there are bumblebees, for example).

⋆ Write a poem about what spring means to you or about a spring theme (gardens, insects, allergies, love?).

⋆ Create a garden report. You could observe the plants in your yard or garden for a week, charting how high they've grown. You might even want to include photographs of their progress. Or write up a list of all the plants you are including in your dream garden (real or imaginary!) and sketch how you want it to look.

* Create a letter poem, using the letters of the word "spring" as the starting point of each line:

  S

  P

  R

  I

  N

  G

* Take photos of things that represent spring. Put the photos in your journal.

* List why you like (or don't like) spring.

* Write down your favorite things to do in spring or imagine an adventure you'd like to have this spring.

* Paint or draw a nature scene, using the great outdoors for inspiration. You can use watercolors, oils, colored pencils, or markers to portray the people, plants, animals, and trees that you see. At this time of year, there's a lot of artistic inspiration all around you.

# From My Journal

*April 22, 1994 (Friday)*

*Dearest Victoria,*

   *Today is Earth Day and I wore my Dad's grizzly bear Earth T-shirt, my bottlecap earrings, and my little bluebird pin. I wrote a splendid poem for Earth Day! It is called: "Gaia, Our Mother." I love it.*
   *The other thing is . . . I think Alec really likes me! We talked and laughed a lot at lunchtime. 'Tis too splendid for words! Well, I have to go read.*

*Love,*
*Jessica*

*P.S. Happy Earth Day!*

# Holiday Fun

* Write a children's story about the Easter Bunny and Easter Egg hunts. Or create a traditional Passover story. Illustrate it, make copies, and staple it together. It would be fun to give the stories away to a little brother or sister, your younger cousins, or any kids you babysit for.

* Write down the oldie-but-goodie trick that you always use on April Fools' Day. Don't forget to play some April Fools' Day tricks on people!

* Celebrate St. Patrick's Day by thinking about things you can do to bring yourself good luck. Do you believe in lucky horseshoes or four-leafed clovers? What are your superstitions?

* For Earth Day, write a poem about the earth or put together a newsletter about saving the environment. Don't stop there—start a Save the Earth club at school, put on a parade that celebrates Earth Day, or send letters to government officials about environmental issues you care about.

# CHECK IT OUT

*KidsShenanigans: Great Things to Do That Mom and Dad Will Just Barely Approve Of* by the Klutz Press Editors (Palo Alto, CA: Klutz Press, 1992). Includes secret codes, simple and complicated tricks, instructions to make paper airplanes, and even a build-your-own whoopee-cushion kit.

*Linnea's Almanac* by Christina Bjork, illustrated by Lena Anderson (NY: Farrar, Straus & Giroux, Inc., 1989). There's also *Linnea in Monet's Garden* and *Linnea's Windowsill Garden.* The three Linnea books have lots of information and beautiful illustrations—they almost make you wish you were Linnea. Learn all about creating your own windowsill garden and almanac. Or imagine that you travel to France like Linnea, who visits art galleries and goes to the garden of the famous artist Claude Monet.

# Dear Reader

*Do you feel good about being a girl? Yes? Well, good—keep smiling and feeling proud. No? Then it's time you did.*

*Women have accomplished many great things and have been pioneers in every field (think of Florence Nightingale, Abigail Adams, Harriet Tubman, Maya Angelou, Indira Gandhi, Sally Ride—the list goes on and on).*

*Did you know that in 1903 a woman (Mary Anderson) invented windshield wipers? That in 1935 a woman (Eva Landman) invented the umbrella? What would daily life (and rainy days!) be without these things?*

*This next section is all about celebrating being a girl. Remember this: Women have changed the world. And you can, too!*

*Love,*
*Jessica*

*"Let her swim, climb mountain peaks, pilot an airplane, battle against the elements, take risks, go out for adventure...."*

Simone de Beauvoir in *The Second Sex*

# Feeling Good About Being a Girl

All girls are unique and special. Whether we're big-boned, skinny, petite, tall, muscular, not-so-muscular, black, white, Asian, Hispanic, Jewish, Catholic, Buddhist, agnostic, etc., or some combination of the above, we hold one thing in common—we're girls (and proud of it!).

There are all sorts of things you can do to celebrate being a girl. Read stories by women authors, or hang out with your friends and listen to songs by female bands like the Indigo Girls or Luscious Jackson. Following are more ideas.

# Celebrate Women

What do Ann Bancroft (polar explorer) and Ella Fitzgerald (jazz singer) have in common? Both were recently inducted into the National Women's Hall of Fame, which is located in Seneca Falls, New York. Even if you can't visit the National Women's Hall of Fame, you can learn more about it from your local library. In your journal, you can write about some of the inductees. (What were their accomplishments? What do you admire about them and their work?)

Did you know that there's a Women's History Month? Celebrated during March, it recognizes the achievements of many famous women. You can celebrate in March (or any other time of year for that matter). Here's how:

* Read books (fiction and nonfiction) about women and girls of the past, present, and future.

* Have a party in March with all your girl-friends. Ask them to dress up as female book characters or famous women in history. (You can order a party-favor pack from the American Girls Collection. Call 1-800-234-1278 and mention order code BBB.)

* Write about women (past and present) who inspire you. Read biographies of their lives or, if available, their published journals. Think about what *you* might do to change the world.

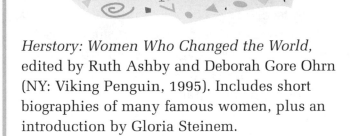

CHECK IT OUT

*Herstory: Women Who Changed the World,* edited by Ruth Ashby and Deborah Gore Ohrn (NY: Viking Penguin, 1995). Includes short biographies of many famous women, plus an introduction by Gloria Steinem.

# Find a Femtor

"Femtor" is the feminist word for mentor.
A mentor is a person who helps you learn and is your friend. It's important to have someone like this to look up to, talk with, and learn from.

Think of someone who could be your femtor: a relative, family friend, neighbor, teacher, or other woman who is interested. If you can't find someone to talk with face-to-face, choose an important historical figure or celebrity you admire. A few good ones to choose are Joan of Arc, Virginia Woolf, Rosa Parks, Marie Curie, or Amelia Earhart. Go to the library to find information about their lives.

Another idea for a femtor is a present-day author you like. Send her letters or postcards in care of her book publisher. (The name of the publisher, and usually the address, are listed on the copyright page of the book.)

Ask the author about her work, her life, and advice she might give you. (TIP: Authors are more likely to respond to letters that are typed or neatly written. Send a self-addressed, stamped envelope so it's easier for them to write back.)

# Go to Work

Every year in April (on the fourth Thursday of the month), the Ms. Foundation for Women celebrates "Take Our Daughters to Work Day." You can participate in the special day by asking your mom to take you to her workplace. If this isn't possible, maybe you could find another woman who can take you to work (your aunt, a family friend, your "femtor," etc.).

The reason this day is important is that it will give you a chance to see what your future job could be like. You'll be able to observe not only your mom but also any other women who work at the same place. Feel free to ask questions and even to help out if possible.

You're not limited to trying this just one day during the year. If you are interested in a particular type of job, call or write to that place of work to see if a female employee might be willing to give you a tour and talk to you about her career. Have a good time and remember—you can be whatever you want to be!

# I Am Every Girl (A Poem)

*If you want to put me*
*into little jars and slap labels on me,*
*you can go ahead and do that.*
*But you must be warned that the jars*
*wouldn't even fit on all the shelves*
*in all the world.*

*I am girlish but I am* **POWERFUL!**

*I am a writer-actress-singer-*
*dancer-painter-scientist.*

*I like computers, trucks, and baseball.*
*I want to hug the world!*

*I am proud of the girl I am now*
*and the woman I am becoming.*

*I am every girl.*

# Journaling Ideas

Historically, women have always kept journals. One reason is that women generally weren't allowed to publish their writings (or, if they did, they often used a man's pseudonym—like George Eliot, whose real name was Mary Ann Evans). Journaling, done in private, was a way for women to write their thoughts, opinions, and feelings.

Celebrate the tradition of women's journaling:

* Find out about one of your female ancestors. Write in your journal about her life and personality. Or make up an adventure story about her, using your imagination.

* Pretend you're a famous woman from another time and place (Cleopatra, Jane Austen, etc.). Write about your life, your typical day, your dreams, and so on.

* Find quotes by famous women to collect in your journal. What do their quotes mean to you? Try writing some sayings of your own that express your personal opinions and your views on life.

# Find Your Own Voice

It's important to let your own voice be heard.
Don't think you can't speak out just because you're
a girl or just because you're a teenager. What issues
are on your mind—the environment, women's rights,
children's rights, violence? You can write about
these things in your journal, but it's also important
to speak out for what you believe in. Here are some
ideas for spreading the word:

* Write to your local or state representatives,
  telling them what issues you stand for.
  A librarian can help you find the addresses
  you need.

* Get your friends together and start an
  Activist Club. You can create posters
  about your cause, write letters to government leaders, and start a petition (get the
  signatures of people who also support
  your cause, then send the petition to the
  attention of officials).

* Publish articles in your school newspaper.
  You can report on the issues or write an
  editorial that states your opinion.

# Sexual Harassment

Let's face it, there are parts of being a girl that aren't always so great. People might judge you by your looks, make rude comments about your body, say you can't do something "because you're a girl," or refer to you by names that are degrading.

This kind of thing has happened to me. Boys have commented on my rear-end, I've had my bra snapped at school, I was paired up with a lab partner who called me a slut, and there have been times when I've been online and people have asked me to tell my bra size or describe what I look like naked. Even thinking about these incidents shakes me up.

Sexual harassment can make you feel angry, confused, stressed-out, and ashamed. If someone harasses you verbally or physically, do not be afraid to tell the person to stop. You can also tell an adult you trust about what happened to you—a parent, teacher, counselor, family friend, or your principal.

Most of all, be proud of your body, your mind, your talents, and everything else that makes you special.

# CHECK IT OUT

*Choices: A Teen Woman's Journal for Self-Awareness and Personal Planning* by Mindy Bingham (Santa Barbara, CA: Advocacy Press, 1993). This is a great planning book for girls ages 13–19, but if you're a mature 11- or 12-year-old, you will probably be ready for it. The book helps you prepare for your future (financially, emotionally, etc.) and builds your self-esteem.

*Girl Power* by Hillary Carlip (NY: Warner Books, Inc., 1995). This book talks about all types of girls—Riot Grrrls, teen mothers, Sorority girls, and beauty queens, plus many others. The author also tells how important it is to write because it empowers you.

*Why It's Great to Be a Girl: 50 Eye-Opening Things You Can Tell Your Daughter to Increase Her Pride in Being Female* by Jacqueline Shannon (NY: Warner Books, 1994). Includes 50 reasons for being proud to be female (ask your mom to read it, too).

# Only Joking

One day three guys were fishing in the ocean. Suddenly one said, "I've caught one and it's a big one, too!" So he reeled in his catch, and it turned out to be a mermaid. She begged them to let her go, saying, "If you release me, I'll grant you each a wish."

The first guy said, "I wish to be two times smarter." The mermaid said, "Done," and the man began quoting Shakespeare perfectly, analyzing each line with extreme insight.

Seeing this, the second guy said, "I want to be three times smarter!" The mermaid said, "Done," and he began to spout out all the answers to questions that had been puzzling scientists and mathematicians for years.

The third guy was so amazed that he said, "I want to be five times smarter!" The mermaid said, "I really think you should reconsider. Wish for anything—a million dollars or anything else!"

Again he said he wanted to be five times smarter. The mermaid replied, "But you'll see the world in a totally different way! You'll feel things you've never felt before!" But the man insisted. So the mermaid sighed and said, "Done."

And he became a woman.

# Girls Online

If you have your own computer (with a modem), or access to one, try exploring the World Wide Web. There are many great sites for girls. Following are some of my favorites. For more information, check out *Net Chick: A Smart-Girl Guide to the Cyberworld* by Carla Sinclair (NY: Owl Books, 1996). If possible, start your very own site.

### Girl Games Homepage
http://www.girlgamesinc.com/

Girl Games is a company that makes computer programs just for girls. On their page you can learn about the company, take a survey, try some brain-bender puzzles, and read a monthly newsletter called *Girls Interwire!*

### Her Online
http://www.her-online.com/

You can post messages, take a survey, participate in an interactive story, and find E-mail pen pals. The site is produced by a company that makes computer programs and games for girls.

### The New Moon Home Page
http://CP.Duluth.MN.US:80/~newmoon/

*New Moon* is the magazine for and by girls. If you like the magazine, you'll love the site! It has articles and information about the magazine. You can even subscribe or submit your own work online.

### The T-room
http://www.troom.com/

This is a site run by Tampax, with all sorts of great stuff for girls. It has information on changes in your body, a pen pal club, places to order free samples, music reviews, games, trivia quizzes, and even an interactive calendar to chart your monthly cycle.

### WomenSpace
http://www.womenspace.com/

Run by the people from The Women's Pharmacy (a catalog of "feminine products," if you know what I mean), this site talks about issues important to girls—without being preachy. You'll learn about changes in your body, sexual choices, products for girls, and so on. There are even some *really* funny jokes.

# Girls' Magazines

There are lots of great periodicals out there that are just for girls. You can get a subscription or take a look at them at your local library. Following are my personal favorites.

### American Girl

This magazine is published by Pleasant Company Publications, which created the American Girls Collection of dolls, books, etc. In every issue you'll find ideas, interesting features, a story about one of the American Girls, and a section that talks about girls' lives in the past.

Write to: Pleasant Company Publications, 8400 Fairway Pl., Middleton, WI 53562, or call: 1-800-234-1278. Check out their new Web site: http://www.pleasantco.com/ag.html

### Girls' Life

Includes ideas, interviews, reviews of music, movies, and books, plus lots of other columns and feature articles. One of the reasons it is so awesome is that it was started by a woman in her 20's, who remembered what it was like when she was a girl and all the magazines she had to read were for and about boys.

Write to: Monarch Avalon Inc., 4517 Harford Rd., Baltimore, MD 21214, or call: (410) 254-9200.

## *The New Girl Times*

This is a great nationwide periodical written for and by girls of all ages, with feature articles, puzzles, poems, and more.

Write to: The New Girl Times, 215 W. 84th St., New York, NY 10024, or call: 1-800-560-7525. They also have an E-Mail address: nugrltim@aol.com

## *New Moon: The Magazine for Girls and Their Dreams*

Published in Duluth, Minnesota, this magazine is edited by a group of girls. Every issue is usually based on a theme or two (such as teachers and teddy bears). The magazine has stories, poems, letters, and drawings from girls around the world.

Write to: New Moon, P.O. Box 3587, Duluth, MN 55803, or call: 1-800-381-4743. See page 125 for the address of their Home Page.

*"I write entirely to find out what I'm thinking, what I'm looking at, what I see, and what it means. What I want and what I fear."*

Joan Didion in *The Writer on Her Work*

# Journaling Can Make You Feel Better

Journals are great listeners when you're sad, angry, or grieving. You can tell your problems and secrets to your journal.

Sometimes when I'm feeling sad or lonely I'll sit in my room, looking out my window, staring at the black, black night. There may not be a star in the sky, but I can see the families cozy in their houses, the cars driving by, and the light tower in the distance. At times like these, I'll listen to some music and write in my journal. Sometimes writing everything down is the first step to feeling better.

# Facing a Problem

Is there a certain problem in your life right now (bad grades, an argument with a friend, worries about the future, etc.)? Write in your journal about how you feel. You can also draw or paint your feelings.

After that, brainstorm ways to solve your problem and make a list of ideas. Draw a picture of how you'll feel once things get better.

# Unsent Letter

If you have something you really want to say to someone but can't, try writing it in a letter (you *don't* have to send it). What you do is get it all out on paper. Maybe it's a letter to your mom and dad, explaining that you're angry about something they did. Or maybe it's a letter to a boy you're interested in but you haven't told him so in person. In the letter, honestly share all your thoughts, all your feelings.

Then read it over. Sometimes, after reading the words on the page, it becomes easier to think about saying them out loud.

# Sisters and Brothers

Sometimes it's really hard to get along with other family members, especially your sisters and brothers. Instead of fighting, try using your journal to sort out frustrations or angry feelings. This can help you to see things more clearly and to figure out what to do.

Sometimes things just build up, and you feel that you need to get away from your siblings. Try to find a private spot to think and write. In your journal, write down the things your sisters and brothers do that bother you or drive you crazy.

After that comes the really challenging part: Write about what you like or love about your sisters or brothers. Sound impossible? Just try to make a list (it can be short, if you want). Think about a time when you laughed or had fun with them. It may help!

# We're Moving?!

Moving to a new town, city, or country can be one of the hardest things you'll go through. I have moved enough times to know this.

When we lived in Pennsylvania and had to move, I cried and cried. There were things I would miss, like the porch outside the window of my bedroom, and the foxes that came to our backyard in the winter, and the summer deer that I sometimes saw—not to mention my friends!

I learned that keeping a journal can be a great help in times like these. You can write about your feelings, descriptions of your house and yard, and anything else that's important to you. Write down all your friends' names and addresses, too.

If you want, you can keep a special photo journal of your hometown: Take photographs of your school, friends' houses, stores you like, the park, and so on, then put a caption or description beneath each picture. You might try finding a partner to keep a Friendship Journal with (for ideas, see pages 96–97).

Every time I've moved (which has been plenty of times), I've made an effort to take photos of my friends, my house, and all my favorite places. I also write down my memories of those favorite places. Getting my friends' autographs is another thing I do.

Then I look over all this stuff and try to memorize it. Some things are too important to ever be forgotten!

It's also important to give the new hometown a chance, so start a journal about your new home. Draw a layout of your new bedroom, for example, or get some information about the town or city you're moving to. Your library is a great resource for this activity, or you can write to the local Chamber of Commerce of your new town for information.

# Your Parents

As you probably know, parents and teenagers can get into some real power struggles. You might argue about money, the clothes you like to wear, doing homework, the people you hang out with, whether to get a job or not, and other things.

One main thing that comes up in my family is that I will want to do something, but my parents won't let me. Or the opposite happens: I don't want to do something, but my parents make me.

This is all part of growing up and getting along in a family. When you have arguments or troubling times, try to work it out as peacefully as possible. My advice is try to talk things out. If you don't want to do something, give your parents good reasons why. Allow them the chance to explain their reasons and feelings, too.

The same goes for situations where you want to do something that your parents aren't sure you should. Let your parents know that you are capable of making choices and decisions, and that you are a responsible person. Then act RESPONSIBLY! (I know, it's easier said than done—but it's important.) If you want to earn your parents' trust, you have to show them you're trustworthy. If you've made a promise, keep it.

# Privacy Contract

Do your parents respect the privacy of your journal? If they secretly read your journal or if they bother you during your personal writing time, you you might try talking to them about it.

If that isn't comfortable for you, write a "Privacy Contract" and sign it with your parents. A contract like this can also work for a brother or sister. Here are some things you might want to say (you can put the contract in your own words):

> *I,* (Your name here), *feel that you do not respect the privacy of my journal. The purpose of this contract is to remind us to respect each other's private time and personal belongings. By signing this form, we are making a promise not to spy or snoop. We are also agreeing that it's okay to spend time alone, as long as we communicate this need beforehand, in a positive and honest way.*

> *Signed* (your name here)

> (name of your parent, guardian, or sibling)

P.S. One last piece of advice: never whine. It will only make things worse. (I should really take my own advice!)

# Saying Good-bye

You may have lost someone in your life. This could be a family member who has died, or a pet. Or maybe your best friend moved away. You may be feeling overwhelmed by your sadness.

Use your journal to help yourself say good-bye and to help work through your sad feelings. You can write down your best memories of the loved one and include photos and any other mementos. Or you can write a good-bye letter. In it, tell the loved one what you're feeling and what he or she has meant to you. You don't ever have to show these writings to anyone, but it might help you and others who are feeling the same sadness. Don't be afraid to talk to someone you love and trust.

## CHECK IT OUT

If you can't talk to someone you know but need help, call this hotline: Boys Town National Hotline (1-800-448-3000). It's not just for boys—it's a youth crisis line for *anyone* to talk about *any* problem. The call is free and won't show up on your phone bill.

# From My Story
## "Phoebe"

*I can't believe I'm actually remembering Grandma Nora without crying. It's so hard. I don't think I'll ever be able to go there without thinking about the times we used to have.*

*At least it's a way to make sure that I'll never forget her. That's what I'm scared of the most—forgetting what she looked like and what her voice sounded like, and all the special things we did together....*

# Friendships

It isn't always easy to get along with your friends, no matter how much you like them. You may find that your friends get on your nerves or act in ways that bother you (putting people down, being bossy, spreading rumors, etc.). Try not to keep your feelings bottled up.

Write in your journal about your friendships and how your friends treat you and others. Are there things you'd like to change about the way one of your friends acts? How? Read over what you've written and decide if you can tell your friend how you feel (remember, be honest but kind).

If you've had a fight with a friend, try to make up. On the next page is a fun recipe for patching things up.

# Salt-Dough "Friendship" Cookies
(These are for sharing, not for eating!)

## Ingredients:

- 2 cups flour
- 1 cup salt
- 1 cup water
- Red food coloring (optional)

## What to Do:

In a large bowl, mix the flour and salt. Slowly add the water. Knead the dough until well mixed. If you want, add a drop of red food coloring. Pat the dough into a thin pancake (about $1/4$ inch thickness), then cut out heart shapes using a heart-shaped cookie cutter (or just use a butter knife). The recipe will make about three dozen hearts.

For each heart, take the butter knife and cut a zig-zagging line down the middle (now you'll have two heart "halves"). With a toothpick, write an "F" on each half to stand for "Friends Forever." Bake the heart halves at 300° for one hour. Keep one side for yourself and give the other to a friend!

> *"Summer days for me*
> *When every leaf is on its tree."*

Christina Rossetti in "Summer"

# Summer
# Journaling

Summer is great for hiking, swimming, and
learning all sorts of interesting things. On
hot days, I love to get an ice-cold glass of
lemonade and a chair, find a shady spot, and
spend hours reading books and writing
in my journal.

Summer is the ideal time for writing because
once school is out, you have a lot more time on
your hands. What better way to spend it than
exploring your thoughts, dreams, and
ideas in your journal?

## Summer Journal Supplies

- Pencils and pens (Summer is wildcard season, so go crazy! Look for any colors that you can find—even neon!)
- Markers, crayons, paints, or colored pencils
- Paper of all colors, sizes, and types (A great resource is Paper Direct. For their free catalog, call 1-800-A-PAPERS.)
- Camera and film
- Glue and scissors
- Postage stamps
- Freedom and imagination!

# Journaling Ideas

* Invent a character and, on various pages in your journal, draw lots of pictures of her (or him, or it) in different poses.

* Write some poetry. Here are several ideas: a poem about the true meaning of summer or about a summer theme (vacations, fireworks, flowers, adventures, hot dogs, watermelon, etc.).

* Don't sit around bored all summer, wishing you were somewhere else. Feel good about where you

live! I am commanding you (well, not really) to go to your local library to find out interesting things about your state. Then write about your findings in your journal. You can even sketch a map of your state, including some of your favorite places and your state's motto, flower, bird, animal, or flag.

* While I'm on the subject of maps, how about a map of YOU? First, draw the outline of your personalized "country" and give it a name (I might call mine "Jessica's World," for example). Include any places that are important to you or even map out your feelings. Make up a motto and flag that tell a little about you.

* Create a letter poem, using the letters of the word "summer" as the starting point of each line:

S
U
M
M
E
R

* Design your "Ultimate Bathing Suit." (Then take photographs of you in the bathing suit that you actually got!)

* Write about an adventure you would like to have this summer. For a variation, write it in the form of a story with you as the heroine.
* List why you like (or don't like) summer.
* If you're stuck at home, make something delightful to take your mind off the hot weather:

## Berry Shake

### Ingredients:

- 1 cup milk
- 2 scoops vanilla ice cream or frozen vanilla yogurt
- Handful of frozen or fresh berries

### What to do:

Place ingredients in a blender; blend until smooth. Enjoy!

# From My Journal

*July 23, 1994 (Saturday)*

*Dear Victoria,*

*In the car on the way to Illinois, I noticed some amazing things in the sky and I wrote them down:*

*"There are lots of big puffy clouds today, perfect for seeing shapes in, but the best of all are the really thin and wispy ones that look like little paint brush-strokes. I saw some that were rainbow colored. Nobody else saw them, it was as though they were put there just for me to see.... I just saw a big cloud with a hole in it. There was a cloud slide coming down from the hole. Was it a slide for angels?"*

*On the way back, when it was dark, I made some other observations: "There are phantom mountains on the horizon tonight. They are purple and hazy and full of wonder and mystery. I am enchanted!"*

*Love,*
*Jessica*

# Holiday Fun

* The last day of school can feel like a holiday! Be sure to take photos of your friends and get their autographs. Glue these into your journal.

* Now that school is out, write your own "school's out" chant (for example, "School's out, school's out, teacher let the fools out...").

* Think or write about the following questions: What is your favorite Fourth of July tradition? What is your favorite thing about this country? What is your *least* favorite thing about this country?

* On the Fourth of July, write a poem about what America means to you.

* Write about a time in American history that fascinates you and research it (at the library, if possible). You can write in any style—a poem, a song, an essay, historical fiction, etc.

* Write about what you would do if you didn't have to go to school ever again. (I hope you don't come up with "watch TV" or "play video games all day." Of course, if those were your favorite activities, I don't think you'd be reading this book.)

* Summer is T-shirt weather, so I thought it would be appropriate to mention them. You can find white T-shirts at just about any store, and they're fun to decorate. Use puffy paints or fabric markers to write your personal message (such as "Yo!") and to get your point across. Add sequins, beads, etc., to decorate it.

* During the long, lazy days of your summer holiday, write letters to your friends and relatives. Here are a few ways to make your letters more creative:

  * Write your message on an inflated balloon, then deflate it (the person who gets it has to blow the balloon up to read the words).

  * Design your own stationery using a computer, your artwork, or some rubber stamps.

  * Write your letter in the form of a story or poem, complete with illustrations. Or write it like a newsletter or zine.

  * You can spice up letters to a best friend or a boy by adding a dab of your signature scent (perfume) or a REAL kiss. (Put on lipstick and kiss the page.)

  * Design a postcard, or just send a cool one from a place you've visited.

- Finally, if you would like more people to write to, try to find information about pen pal programs—your local library can help. Or send a self-addressed, stamped envelope to:

> Friends Forever PenPals
> Friends Communications
> P.O. Box 20103
> Park West Station
> New York, NY 10025

*Amelia's Notebook* by Marissa Moss (Berkeley, CA: Tricycle Press, 1995). When a young girl (Amelia) has to move, her mom buys her a notebook to write her thoughts in. There's a lot of humor and great illustrations—fun summer reading!

*Alice in Between* by Phyllis Reynolds Naylor (NY: Dell Publishing Company, Inc., 1996). This book is just great! It's a story about Alice and her friends and their triumphs, trials, and adventures while growing up. When you read this story, you will swear that Ms. Naylor spied on your life (which just proves she's an excellent author).

*Hey World, Here I Am!* by Jean Little (NY: HarperCollins Children's Books, 1990). This is a collection of poems and observations about life, friendship, family, identity, and love, as if from the journal of a teenager named Kate.

# A Few Last Words

This may be the end of this book, but I hope it's not the end of your journaling. If you've been journaling while you were reading, then you know how wonderful and important and fun it is, and you'll probably want to keep doing it for the rest of your life. If you've been reading this book to find out if journaling is for you, then I hope the answer is yes. Write on!

Remember, never stop writing.
Everything you write,
everything you think
and say, is important.

## You are important!

# Read More About Journaling

If you like writing in a journal, here are some good books to read. They offer ideas, writing tips, and encouragement to anyone who is trying to keep a journal or who dreams of becoming a published writer.

*A Book of Your Own: Keeping a Diary or Journal* by Carla Stevens (Boston, MA: Houghton Mifflin Company, 1993). Includes wonderful excerpts from a variety of people's journals.

*Life's Companion: Journal Writing as a Spiritual Quest* by Christina Baldwin (NY: Bantam Books, Inc., 1991). The author talks about her childhood, shares journal excerpts, and tells how to get in touch with your spiritual nature.

*The New Diary: How to Use a Journal for Self-Guidance and Expanded Creativity* by Tristine Rainer (NY: Jeremy P. Tarcher, Inc., 1979). This book is old, but you can probably find it at your library (it got me started on journaling when I found it at a library book sale for fifty cents). It's great for learning about yourself.

*Real Toads in Imaginary Gardens: Suggestions and Starting Points for Young Creative Writers* by Stephen P. Policoff and Jeffrey Skinner (Chicago, IL: Chicago Review Press, Inc., 1991). Includes many creative, helpful tips and exercises for young writers.

*Writing—A Fact and Fun Book* by Amanda Lewis (Reading, MA: Addison-Wesley Publishing Company, Inc., 1992). Explores the history of writing and has activities such as making your own quill pen or book.

*Writing Down the Days: 365 Creative Journaling Ideas for Young People* by Lorraine M. Dahlstrom (Minneapolis, MN: Free Spirit Publishing, Inc., 1990). A whole year's worth of journaling ideas, plus fun facts about famous people, historic events, and even holidays you've probably never heard of.

*Writing for Your Life: Discovering the Story of Your Life's Journey* by Deena Metzger (San Francisco, CA: Harper San Francisco, 1992). Includes lots of ideas for developing your creativity, spirituality, and writing, and it suggests keeping a journal.

*The Young Person's Guide to Becoming a Writer* by Janet E. Grant (Minneapolis, MN: Free Spirit Publishing, Inc., 1995). Offers tips, advice, and encouragement to young writers who are serious about starting a writing career and finding a publisher.

NOTE: All of these books offer great ideas for your journal or writing career. If you are serious about your writing and want feedback from other people, try starting a writer's group (at home or school), asking your parents or teachers for comments on your writing, or signing up for a writer's course at school, at your nearby library, or at a local organization for writers. Good luck!

# Index

## A

Activities for journaling, 66–81.
*See also* Fall journaling; Spring journaling; Summer journaling; Winter journaling
Alcott, Louisa May, 10, 23, 45
American Anorexia/Bulimia Association, 55
*American Girl* (magazine), 126
*Anne Frank: The Diary of a Young Girl* (Frank), 13
"Anne of Green Gables" series (Montgomery), 45
Anorexia, 54–55
Appearance, 53
April Fools' Day, 109
Art
    journals, 92–93
    supplies, 6
Autobiography, 18
Autumn journaling. *See* Fall journaling

## B

Berry shake (recipe), 144
Birth control, 63
Birthdays, 72
Body changes, 49–65, 121
Boys, 48
Boys Town National Hotline, 136
Brothers. *See* Siblings
Bulimia, 54–55

## C

Campfire stew (recipe), 33
Christmas, 8, 86–87, 88–89
Codes, writing in, 46
Collages, 15, 88
Comic strips, 70
Coming-of-age ceremonies, 58

Companion, for journaling, 70
Computers
    journals, 94–95
    software, 75
    Web sites, 124–125
Conversation. *See* Dialoguing
Cookies, soft-dough friendship (recipe), 139
Covers, designing, 68
Creativity. *See* Activities

## D

Dialoguing, 39
Disguised writing, 46
Dreams, 24–25

## E

E-zines, 95
Earth Day, 109
Easter, 109
Eating disorders, 54–55

## F

Fall journaling, 28–35
    ideas, 30–31
    story ideas, 35
    supplies, 30
Family journals, 100–101
Feelings, and journaling, 128–139
Femtors. *See* Mentoring
Fighting, and journaling, 131
Filipovic, Zlata, 12, 13
Fourth of July, 146
Frank, Anne, 12, 13, 50, 104
Free-writing, 38
Friends Forever PenPals, 148
Friendships, 138
    journals, 96–97

Pregnancy, 63
Premenstrual syndrome (PMS), 56–57
Privacy, 8–9
    contract, 135
Puberty, 56–57

## R

Reading, 26
Recipes, 26, 33, 47, 139, 144
Respect, and sex, 63
Review, 44
Rules for journal-keeping, 4

## S

St. Patrick's Day, 109
Sample journal entries, 14, 32, 59,
    86–87, 103, 108, 137, 145
School's-out journals, 80–81, 146
Scrapbooks, 88, 98–99
Seasons. *See* Fall journaling; Spring
    journaling; Summer journaling;
    Winter journaling
Secret codes, 46
Self-esteem, 1, 27
Sex, 61–63
Sexual harassment, 121
Sexually transmitted diseases
    (STDs), 63
Siblings, 131
Sisters. *See* Siblings
Software, 75
Spring journaling, 104–110
    ideas, 106–107
    supplies, 106
STDs. *See* Sexually transmitted
    diseases (STDs)
Story groups, 77
Story ideas, 23, 35
Stream-of-consciousness writing, 38
Summer journaling, 98, 140–149,
    ideas, 142–144
    supplies, 142

## T

Take Our Daughters to Work Day, 117
Tape recorders, 6, 8
Thanksgiving, 33–34
Time to journal, 7, 44
Time travel, 46
Tips, 7, 15
Trading cards, 71

## V

Valentine's Day, 89
Values, 20–21
Voice, finding your own, 120

## W

Web sites. *See* World Wide Web sites
Weight, 54–55
Winter journaling, 82–89
    ideas, 84–85
    supplies, 84
Wishes, 22
Women
    celebrating, 114–115
    joke, 123
    and journaling, 111–127
World Wide Web sites, 94, 95,
    124–125
Writing
    opposite hand, 38
    utensils, 6
    writer's block, 37
    writer's journals, 102

## Z

Zines, 74–76, 95. *See also*
    Magazines; Newsletters
*Zlata's Diary* (Filipovic), 12–13